Bone Circle

Bone Circle

Poems by

Susan Roney-O'Brien

Cover photograph: Philip O'Brien.
Cover design: Shay Culligan

ISBN: 978-1-949229-43-1

Kelsay Books
Aldrich Press
www.kelsaybooks.com

For Hugh, Frances and Stephen

Acknowledgments

"Finding my Mother" *Ekphrasis*
"Forsythia" *The Worcester Review*
"My first language" *Potato Hill Poetry*
"My father's jaw" *Echo & Spark*
"Virga" *Echo & Spark*
"Widdershins" *Periphery: Southern Revival*
  Deep Magic for Hurricane Relief

Contents

Heeling In

Disclaimer

It began in a small town—
neighbors whiter than churches
    Were you poor?
Of course, we used to wait
at Goodwill boxes.
    You mean you went through them,
    took stuff?
Well, just what we needed.
Nobody saw us.
    Must have been hard.
Not really. We were a typical
family. Father worked two jobs, drank a bit.
Mom at home. Both parents smoked.
We went to church
    What kind of kid were you?
Quiet. I stuttered, so learned not to bother talking.
I wrote and passed poems off as someone else's.
    Really?
It was safer not to admit.
    So you lied.
I guess you could say that.
What I came to you about, in fact, is poetry, the lies in it.
    You lie in your poems?
Just about situations, experiences that speak to me,
experiences I can get inside of and manipulate.
    You even change the stories you steal?
I make them better. You could say
I customize them to fit my needs.
    So what do you want from me?
    Wait a minute,
    did you take something that happened to me
    and turn it into a poem?
Yeah. I was wondering how to tell you. Your life is my life.
In fact, everybody's life is my life.
    So you're a liar and a thief.
Just so you know.

Widdershins

Midden

In all archaeological digs, everyday waste—
shards of glass, slivers of wood, fabric
matted and sprung full of holes—tells the truth,
a detritus trail attesting to what you hope
would never be found,
what you chose against remembering,
resisted to recall, but
insists on surfacing.
Once glimpsed, you can't turn away.
The residue fills your sanctuaries, bars exits.
You begin with fragments,
almost recollected images—
a stain on the carpet, grey light
in the upstairs hall
where ivy wallpaper
forms devil faces,
and now you're in position, stand outside
the room where darkness has collected
among webs you've always feared.
Once you wrench off hinges and shoulder through,
your brother's death illuminates
the abandoned so long sealed
that mold's litmus ears bend out
from where they've grown
between joists, beams—
rubbery, deaf, like flesh but cold—
and you must dig them all away
to get to what lies behind.
You drag the chisel home; blade abrades
skin, chafes flesh, exposes dolls, headless
in the closet, outgrown snakeskin
sewn into the binding of your family Bible,
that plaster cast of a dead child's hand,
dark windows braced with knuckle bones.

The Setting

First the pipe—
a straight-stemmed Kaywoody briar with a scorched bowl—
in the ashtray on the arm of the chair,
a case of Ballantine. No rug.
At the right—a brick fireplace, the firebox black.
The chair, gray Naugahyde with jagged pencil holes
outlining a daisy shape on the seat. A staircase.
As I start downstairs, my bare feet slapping the treads,
my father looks up: I tell him the hall outside my room
is papered with faces of the dead.
He stares. I am a child and do not know any better.

The Tin

From the cabinet above the Formica counter
I pull down the blue Edgeworth box, shake its dry bones
close to my ear—either someone had placed small beads inside
or my father was telling the truth—
and when I get bored with the tight rectangular tin,
open it: tail of a rattler,
five, no, six translucent segments.

1953, Boston

We came from the country, climbed white stairs
that smelled of pee, twenty-six steps
and Momma and Poppa didn't let me stop once.
They said we had to hurry;
the mean old man was dying.

Grandfather lay in a wide room, walls grey,
windows shut tight, bottles like small glass soldiers,
lined along table edges, upright. A clock chimed twice
and a lady came in, lifted his head, spooned
red medicine in without saying anything.

He looked like the snapping turtle
my father dragged off our path
who clenched the stick he used to pull her.
Grandfather bit the spoon but didn't move or speak,
just kept his lips closed, teeth clamped.

Dust motes floated onto white blankets.
Momma took his hand but he shook her off
and Poppa said, "Let's go. He doesn't care,
doesn't know his own daughter.
We need to let the dog out."

When we left, I sat in the wayback
and waved. We sang *Row, row, row your boat*
all the way home except for Momma. She
scrunched close to the window,
her back shaking, until we stopped at our yard.

Face in the Window

You were already there—
in the breakfast room window
of our new house, far away from uncles and aunts,
your ordinary brown hair curving around your face
like the hands of a saint no one has named—
I wanted to say: I know you,
you are the reason we came.
When you waved me away,
I stood on my tiptoes, banged on the door
and my mother emerged,
her plain brown hair sparking red,
so I gave you up easily,
the way you came.

Forsythia

From the hall I watched him shatter the orange dishes
my mother thought unbreakable—
slamming them against grey tile
as she crouched, denying milkman, mailman,
all who came to the house while he was at work,
who heard quick breaths between her words,
appraised her body.

Each night
I set the table and when it was time
we all sat for him to lead us in grace,
careful to keep our elbows off the cloth,
careful to eat everything so he wouldn't say
how ungrateful we were for the food on our plates
and then, with his leather belt, teach us manners.
But when he smashed those dishes I ran.

It was still light so it must have been spring,
yes, May, because I crawled through wands
supple as whips but studded with blossoms
to get inside the forsythia cave.
I looked as hard as I could:
each stem was a tight green throat,

each mouth tongueless gold entered by bees
whose furry bodies spun back out
dusted with pollen,
                    and watching them
I almost forgot the sounds inside the house
until my mother slammed the windows down
and my ears filled with buzzing.

Huddled in the damp earth beneath forsythia,
straining for silence, I watched night

billow up from the dirt, sapping the flowers.
When the crashes stopped,
she called for me: *Come in Come in.*

The High Mirror

To see I climb the toilet lid, slide
onto the sink rim. Nights I dream
myself tall, grackle-gloss hair,
high cheek-boned face, dark skin,
and from anthracite eyes,
can see caves that lead
to the center of the earth.

But each morning the same
blonde, blue-eyed, girl
stares back.

One Bath

I fill the tub with rose petals, plucked
"love me, love me not"
from Mother's prize bushes
and slide my body in,
lie back, imagine
Guinevere dreaming
her Lancelot, then
my brother needs to go
and I have to get out,
disappear the petals,
not let them clog the drain, not
get my father up here
in his steel-toed workboots
a plunger in his fist, snake
coiled against his chest.

Visiting Chicago

Tall grey stairs led to a porch where a woman older than wheels
sat in a rocker and sang me salvation, "One two, three, four, five,
six, seven, all good children go to heaven," and I snuggled in her
lap, wondered if I were good enough, if hating could keep me out.
I hated my Uncle George and Uncle George was going to Hell. I
knew that. He was the youngest of twelve—three years older than
me—my father's little brother who carried Snow, my white cat,
into the dirt basement, pelted her with stones, rolled her broken
body in a towel and left it in my bed.

What Fairy Tales Do

Was it Sinbad or some other hero
who strode over burning coals?
                              It wasn't me
who tried it after grownups holed up inside
eating strawberry ice cream and drinking beer.

I was three—believed all the stories ever read me,
slept knee bent like a ballerina, arms
beneath the blankets, and I would lie still
so the witches at my window would not see
that I was breathing, a living child.

It wasn't me. Two steps in, I screamed.
My father ran out, picked me up, carried me inside.
                              I cried
when they stuck my feet in a pan of ice. I cried
when my soles puffed up then split.
I cried when my great grandmother wrapped them in gauze
and I had to sit near her and say prayers all day
instead of climbing the big oak tree.

The Girl Upstairs

In the middle of dinner
when I can't eat any more
and the Armenians are still starving
and still Armenian,
the girl upstairs
slips my Sunday dress
over her head,
leaving shorts and
stained jersey in a pile
by the end of my bed
in the room I share with two sisters,
pulls yellow curls back
straight, smiles at herself
in the mirror on the wall
and runs to the dining room
jangling bracelets
my brother brought me
home from the carnival.
My mother smiles
and greets her
using my name
as she slides into my chair.

I was sitting there.

Migraine

My mother lies on her side
on the davenport,
her ear blocked by the fold
of her arm, an afghan over
her face. I build bunks of benches
for my sisters, lay dolls
in each sleeping place so
they lie safe
and my small sisters
won't try to climb onto
the shaky beds.

The three of us
let our babies sleep and
take oranges from the crisper,
balance them onto plates.
I peel each one
make long streamers of skins
and we begin, break
each sphere into sections,
slip pieces
into our mouths until
Mother lifts the afghan
from her shoulders, slides
into a sitting position,
and stands.

The youngest takes
one hand, the other holds
her leg. I fold the afghan, tuck
it into the corner of the couch
and get another plate
from the pantry,
place an orange on the dish.

Our mother unfolds
a napkin onto her lap,
opens her lips.

Door

I sneaked into his room
when my brother was at baseball,

opened the closet door and stood on the stool
he must always have used.

One cupboard opened onto the other
into the bathroom.

My mother didn't believe me when I told
that he watched me from there

but even through my Ivory Soap gargle,
he knew I knew.

Widdershins

Inside a cottage in the middle of my town
Miss Bell and King were always old and I
was little though I didn't think so then, and
would go see her in her funny house with
the pantry full of jars, the black
woodstove, the root cellar and the few
steps between the parlor and the rooms
upstairs. Her yard was all flowers and out
back two poles laced with ropes held wet
clothes and the clothespins weren't like
my mother's but old ones she said her
father carved at night. She knew magic
and told me not to walk on the other side
of the laundry pole from her or else I'd
have to go around widdershins to undo the
spell that would divide us. All spring I
visited and King never barked at me. Then
she paid my brother to get her a TableTalk
pie and by mistake he dropped it and Miss
Bell asked my mother to buy a new one
but my ma said no because the pie wasn't
wrecked just caved in. Next day Ma told
me never to visit Miss Bell again and
when school began and I walked by her
house every day King would growl
and the curtains move.

Roadkill

"Watch this," he said, wiffle-headed, eight,
the school nurse's son, and slunk to the edge
of Pleasant Street, dumped ketchup
over his checkered shirt,
pulled a clump of play money
from his pocket and scattered it
into the gutter where he lay
on his back, the red pooling
near his chest, one arm flung out.
The baby blue station wagon
came on—an old man peering
through the windshield—

and the money blew in the road,
flattened itself against the bumper
as the car braked and Billy Boy or
Bobby, or whatever his name was, writhed.
The old man hobbled toward him,
his face white as the pickets
around the boy's front lawn
and when he got just close enough,
the kid flipped onto his side,
pulled a squirt gun from his pocket
and got 'im.

After dark

when one sister was getting her bath, I would slip down the stairs
past my father's chair and out the screen door to the backyard. The
Russians had just put Sputnick into space, fixed it so it would cross
our town's sky every night. I'd run across the grass, whistle up the
twins who lived next door and we'd lie on our backs and watch
the one white eye we were sure could see everything pass while
stars and moon stood still. And after, when the universe righted
itself, we would pick out old favorites—Big Dipper, Cassiopeia,
Orion—our pillars in the night sky—those and the north star that
would steer us home, should we ever go anywhere. Sometimes,
lying on my back in the grass, I would pretend I was clinging to
the edge of the world and would fall, spiral up or down, whatever
direction held the sky, into the dark, into what I knew was deep
and wide and unknown if I dared let go.

Fire

Smoke climbs my grandfather's stairs.
The city bleeds flame.
Outside the gate a dog cries, crows flatten
shadows into apple blossoms,
blackbirds land, wing bars like lips, red and yellow.
Next year at this time contrails will etch the sky.
Flight is the earth moving around a soon-to-be
snuffed-out star. Can you feel the world's slow turning?
When the last building burns, bees will hive in the rafters,
build octagonal cells. Take my hand;
smoke washes through you into the cellar hole
filled with water.

Polio

When I was in first grade,
pools closed
and even the five wild children
from the faded brown ranch
in the development
stayed in their own yard.
At church everyone prayed
for the afflicted which I thought
was somewhere near Armenia
where my father always said
children were starving.

The biggest boy
in Mrs. Clark's first grade
rode his bike all the way,
even across Main Street until
the day he had to go home;
his legs were stuck,
and Carol came only one day
and moved to a metal drum
where she lay while
her grandmother
sang her the ABC's.

School closed. My best friend
moved away. The first
May Saturday every kid
waited in line
on the town hall steps
not touching anybody
and drank paper cup medicine.

Hurricane

My swing swings without me
under the grape arbor
and then   quiet.

If I hurry, Momma says,
I won't be late for school
so slickered, umbrellaed

I trot up Miller, cross Main,
go down Upland, over
to North

and follow the road to school.
The sign on the big front door
says *NO SCHOOL HURRICANE*

and I scurry toward home
past the library, down
Pleasant

and the wind inside-outs
my umbrella. It was the eye
Momma says

when I get home
wet, curls blown
like a dandelion puff.

Then catalpa limbs thrust
through green storm windows,
shatter glass, splinter frames.

At the corner of the house
forsythia conducts a wind ballet
all its wands going at once so

we huddle in the back hall singing
because Momma says
hurricanes hate singing.

and when Daddy comes home
he hugs everyone
even my brother.

The Acrobat

Best time is just before dinner
when Mother cooks, brother
watches TV and my sisters
squabble on the porch.
I turn the silver knob,
shut white bathroom door.

I take off everything except
underpants, arch forward, fling
my legs up as hands land flat
against black and white
linoleum, see bottoms of things,
pipes, handles. From the two
high windows, yellow light
falls onto discarded clothes.

Again and again I
turn the world on its head
to try to figure out how
everything is put together,
to find a safe place
both apart from
and inside my family.

The Way

Bottom-sitter in the skiff
between Father's soles
and Mother's sandaled feet
reads a fairy tale wherein
the princess leaves the kingdom,
tames a black-backed jackal
and takes from it the desolation
of abandoned hearth stones.
She teaches her creature words,
language that greys into mist,
divides parents from child,
blears truth with myth. Clouds
shackle the sun.

But she who is now princess
understands that all creatures speak,
and words link souls together,
forge chains of responsibility.
The story gains momentum.
The jackal learns to weep
when he speaks from his heart,
and dies from weeping.
The princess child
who taught him
makes her way alone.

Brother Door

Crook

If you're going to walk
into the past, you need
to at least start grounded,
and carry a stick that could serve
as a cudgel, should you need it
to beat back regrets,

a stick to wedge doors open
while you slick your hair,
make yourself presentable
to the long dead, the put-aways
you never thought
you'd have to face again,

a once-living stick, a part
of what went before. Best
if you carve it yourself. Use
what is there. Oak is strong;
bone's often brittle, smashes
itself rather than the ghosts
it's battling.

But if bone is all you have,
leastwise wash off the gore.
A splash of bleach won't hurt
to wipe out latent connections
to the living. You need to
start out clean, smooth,

so nothing catches, nothing
slows you down. Make sure
it's straight when you site
down the length, straight to the eye;
a twisted stick will simply lead you
back to where you didn't want
to start.

Destined for Greatness

Our young mother, anesthetized as in those days,
pushed you out, veiled, in the caul,
that amnion promise of good luck, second sight,
protection from death by drowning.

It might have been what saved your eye,
when you fell on a saw blade at six-years-old,
and all that marked you was a saw-tooth scar
between eye and brow and Father's vow

to keep you from tools no matter
how your hands ached to pound a hammer
or plane a board smooth.

Mother believed in portents and signs:
at eight, a white line clear as a rope
circled your neck in the class picture,
a cleric's collar, she called it, and smiled,

proud we'd have a priest in the family.
She enrolled you in Catholic school,
bought a piano you could learn to play,
at night prayed with you first.

When we'd fight, I'd get spanked. You'd
be sent to your room to *reflect*, the caul
your talisman, saving you from punishment.

You were good. I stuttered,
choked into poetry. You toed the line,
followed the assigned path, head raised,
green eyes blazing, lips praising the Redeemer.

One Saturday in the Old House

A kitchen chair, back-turned against the sink
and Father bends to test the water.
I am three, his first daughter, and this
ritual is what we share before
the weekly fight begins—
his square fingers work Breck into my curls.
He does not sing or tell me stories.
He washes my hair and rubs it dry.

My brother, stripped to shorts,
holds the boxing gloves,
a quarter orange between his teeth and waits
running in place until Daddy rinses the sink
and moves the chair against the wall.
Mother rings the old brass bell and the boxers
touch gloves beneath the circline light.
My brother jabs with his right,
his six-year-old fist deflected with a turn.

Daddy laughs but the boy keeps on—
punches his stomach and his thighs,
scampers sideways when Daddy tries to hit him.
Momma's watching close and laughing.
Daddy's eyes squint thin as knife blades
and he swipes my brother's cheekbone,
smashes his ear with the other hand.

Momma screams. She rings the bell.
But Daddy pounds my brother
until he drags himself outside.

Before the screen door slams,
Momma runs to find him. Daddy cries.
I crawl into the parlor, crouch inside the fireplace,
paint my face with ashes and I hide.
My father comes to find me.
He washes my hair again and rubs it dry.

My first language

was not words but
hesitations. Caught beneath
the needle, song
skips, repeats a phrase,
slips back,
repeats—
each word a fishbone
coughed into white bread
at my parents' dinner table
where my father intones,
"Think twice, speak
once," and I cannot
get my mouth to open
at all.

I sit—unable
to finish cold peas,
mashed potatoes—
silent. By the time
I want to break
through the circle
both words and most family
have gone—

my brother to homework,
sister to our room—
but Mother and I,
waiting for me
to finish the food or ask
to be excused, face each other

from opposite sides of the table
in the dark.

Runaway

I walked the silversleek steel bones between back yards
and woods when I ran away from home the first time,
balanced on the rails until vibrations pulsed me down
and I leaped off and ran as far as I could so my mother
wouldn't find me, wouldn't make me come home.

And this was almost all and I was almost somewhere else
when a train came fast—all stutter and gleam—and I dove
for the weeds beside the tracks, hoping I jumped far enough
to not get sucked under the wheels. I landed on a log.
At least that was what it felt like—that spotted dog I hugged—

the one with both his eyes gone.

Brock's Field

The net sewn from cheesecloth
threaded onto a wire coat hanger bent into a circle,
the circle duct taped to a dowel about
three feet long

and the white cloth billowed as I ran
hugging the book that rubbed against my chest.
Bring one home, my mother shouted,
the killing jar in her hand.

I crossed the road where meadow grasses—
little blue stem, rye—bent among Joe Pye weed
just beginning to pink, and settled in,
The Girl of the Limberlost

open, sun dappling the page, grasshoppers, spittlebugs,
even praying mantises surrounding me as I lay
in the field, lost in the story, and waved the net
occasionally to signal my mother

who was surely looking out the kitchen window
to check that I was chasing them, checking
that I was not doing what I always did,
read, sprawled across

flattened grasses, the fragile, short-lived
butterflies safe and sailing in blue air.

Reader

By second grade when we sound the letters out,
the teacher listening her way around the circle
hardly makes anyone say each distinct letter,
connecting them in a spoken dot-to-dot,
they had gotten so good
at slurring sounds into words.
The last to read, I count paragraphs down: How many
p's and b's and s's lie like snares to snarl my tongue?

Hunched over, sweating
in the too-tight dotted Swiss my mother made, I try
to concentrate on the hard edge of the chair
biting into my thighs, a fly circling—
and I lean behind the curtain of hair, reading ahead—
the words a waterfall, smooth and straight, flowing
uninterrupted, and the sun glints rainbows off the spray
and I hear myself say all the words,
                                    then she points at me
and nothing can hide me, nothing can
save me: "The b-boy ran p-past the gray rock," I say
and the others tap their feet and snicker.

Sacrosanct

In third grade I know:
blankets are to cover,
bed is for sleep;
my brother is supposed
to slip through our room,
creep into his own
without stopping,
without waking
the toddler
or the baby in the crib,
not crouch at the foot of my bed
against shell pink eaves
and between closet and night
lift the covers.

And the priest had spoken.
He said each body
is a temple of God—
sacrosanct was the word
he said from the altar
and I looked it up
so I would know
and kept that word
tight between my thighs
so each time
my brother went by
I clenched it close
and lay as though
asleep.

Remember

It was Pride my sister swallowed, the furniture polish Ma kept under the sink, and I watched her crawl toward the cabinet, open the door and drink, thinking I'd never do that, and went back to mixing up the brownies with Ma. When my sister started to gag, my mother saw the half-empty bottle and called the police. She held her in her arms saying she wasn't getting away—after all the blue baby bills, the year in Children's Hospital, the oxygen tent in the living room. Then she told the ambulance men I'd be fine alone and they left. I opened the stove and put the brownies in, knowing how proud Ma would be when she got home, but when she called and I told her, she didn't remember we were making brownies, just said she and my sister would be back in a while. I hung up the phone, climbed down from the counter and waited for the timer to buzz.

Losing Faith

It begins between
call and response on a Sunday morning
in autumn. I am eleven and my sisters
seven and three and the younger one
carries the feet of a pheasant
our father bagged the day before
in her church-coat pocket. The priest
has just left Latin and even I
understand what he says
without the secret language
on one side of the hymnal
and he says, "The Lord be with you"
just as Molly pulls the pheasant feet
out and shoves them into Carrie Anne's face—
she who had just received her first
communion, whose hair was always brushed,
knees unscuffed—and both sisters
tear down the center aisle toward the door,
the younger yelling, "Peasant feet! Peasant feet!"
Our mother genuflects, grabs my hand
while the congregation drones on undisturbed
as though pheasants and little girls
have no place in their stained glass
and plaster world.

Spring, 1957

Allowed to play just one,
you chose baseball, your team
named after the Boston Braves;
that's how long ago it was,

and I, your little sister,
at practices, never during games,
would jump from the bleachers,
scream, *bury me with roses,*

before I fell safe, unbroken
to trampled grass. You played
shortstop, sometimes pitcher,
but your throws were never

fast enough or cast to avoid
the bat. But, boy, could you run,
and the last time I saw you hit,
bases loaded, the ball

on fire, a meteor smoking
through the air, flew out to left field
where Bobby Cummings leapt
but couldn't catch it before

it flared over the fence. I swear
as soon as you swung, you ran
and by the time the ball was gone
you were home and fallen

onto the plate. You lay there
until the coach helped you up,
carried you to the dugout,
put you down. Our mother

climbed from the stands,
stumbled to her friend's car
with you in her arms, rode
home and called the doctor.
He sidelined you.

The Last I Heard

My brother stepped down, headed
to the cellar where he had to move
after I threaded rope along porch windows
while everyone but me was gone,
and hung sheets the entire neighborhood
could see, bumped bed, bureau downstairs,
out of the room I shared with two sisters.

I had breasts coming, and my brother
had to cut through our room to get to his.

Just curiosity, my mother said. My father
dropped his beer bottle into the case
and walked onto the porch where I lay
reading. *Nice place you got here,* he said,
but no heat. Tough sleeping winters.
Next morning he measured basement walls
for wallboard, bought floor tile
for my brother's new room.

Stringed Instrument

A Steinway coerced into the corner and my brother at it,
glaze-eyed, fingers splayed. I sit in my father's chair,
legs draped over the side, feet thumping air.
My brother can't read music, but says
it's inside his head and if he doesn't
get it out of there, he'll go crazy.

I'm old enough to think I know how crazy feels; it starts
with confetti in the eyes and a knife to the skull.
Lights scream and bile rises in my throat
like a shriek I can't recognize as mine.
When I tell my brother, he smiles,
That's migraine, he says.

Mine is genius. I swing my foot into where his eyes would be
if he were sitting closer, facing me. He pummels
the keys. I think about the piano strings
inside, how tight the pull must be,
how carefully adjusted so each
vibrates compatibly like

he and I are supposed to in our family.

Answers

Hidden behind the school bus park
safe within Indian grass, deer tongue,
fox hedge, praying mantises
turn their heads all the way around,
and I know magic. The wind
answers questions, but God
wasn't working by the time I was ten.

At Sunday mass, Father Corcoran talked
miracles over Miss Stuart's feathered hat.
Her lace-up shoes on stubby feet
thumped the edge of the pew,
legs straight out from under her black dress;
she couldn't reach the floor.

Father Corcoran couldn't make her grow
and Tommy in the children's row—
strange what you remember—
grew tall but never
could count past nine. I decided
thinking about sin kept people small.

In the meadow, net-winged midges
hover, cardinals glide,
spiders weave veils finer
than any on a grandmother's hat.
Lightning bugs bring stars
down to size.

I ask the wind
if I'll ever understand why
God chooses to live inside
where priests cry sin and hell-fire,
when outside, in fields no one tends,
orioles sing, black-eyed Susans
blossom and sway.

No Matter How I Felt Around

My friend, younger than me,
said there were three.
I could find only the two I knew.
She said she'd found another
and I'd just have to wait; I'd see

and I was simply sitting
on the toilet seat, starting to pee
when roses dropped, one
after another into clear water.
What would become of me?

Coming of Age

School mornings I'd stop,
walk past the parlor, stand
by your mother in front of the stove.
She'd call you down and we'd go,
join the other kids on the road.

After, we'd practice pidgin ballet,
don your big sister's clothes,
strut a fantasy runway,
wave black ostrich feather fans,
dance up and down the stairs.

Every Saturday I'd help clean your room
until the day a new friend called.
I heard you say she could come over
when your maid went home.
I stopped coming then,

took the long way to school alone.
Sometimes though, I'd walk by your house
and wonder what would have happened
if I hadn't heard that call, but by then
you were gone from me

and when I heard that your mother
who used to count my curls had slit her wrists
in the tub one morning and you
were the one who found her,
I didn't say anything.

Miller and Oak

When the car hit my little sister, she lay on the pavement in front of my house and the woman who hit her looked at her watch, said she was late. My mother picked my sister up and slid her into the back seat, said, "I'm calling the police and then you'll drop us off at the hospital. I don't drive." I stood by the side of my road where I had seen green leaves swell and bloom within a day, thinking the woman would drive away with my sister in her car, that she'd drive away before the police came and take my sister and we didn't even know her name.

Dressing Down

My mother's round-toed, black suede, fat-heeled pumps,
her double-breasted suit, shoulder pads, gridiron-thick,
jacket nipped at the waist, straight skirt—
she was a flirt in the forties, worked retail
then took up nursing, all those boys come home from war.
She stored old clothes in cardboard bins in the big closet,
key squirreled behind her wedding photo on the mantel,
and when the clothes fit, I wore them to school until
I discovered Auschwitz, Treblinka, their raw-boned survivors,
saw films of gaunt bodies, striped rags flapping.
My mother, low-voiced, said she didn't know
about the camps, nobody would have believed it anyway,
but I put back her clothing, read everything I could find,
decided everyone must have known—the smoke rising,
ghosts of six million dead on its breath. I wouldn't buy
striped outfits, wore clothes that reminded me
of nothing, clothes without a past.
I wish I could say I rose up in anger. Instead, silent, I
wrote nightmares into notebooks, rode my bike
no hands, read fantasies, fairytales,
and when America moved on to my war, I wore
jeans and flannel, black work boots,
but didn't understand why my brother was arguing
with his friends about napalm, draft cards, Canada
until I saw a photograph of a girl younger than me,
naked, running, her scream in my throat.

Visit

We turn at the nurse's station
into a room where an old man
faces the wall in a harness, a strap
binding his waist to the chair.
My mother raises his chin
where a scar gathers the flesh in a puckered seam.
I look away. Outside the dumpster overflows:
snarled gauze, incontinence pads,
garbage in plastic bags heaped above
green metal sides. A gull straddles the rim,
pokes through a bag and flies off, squawking.
"He can't talk," my mother says. I step closer:
the old man lifts a hand—not in greeting
but to close it over his jaw. He finds
a stranger's face with vaguely familiar eyes.
I watch the hand reach mine, hold it palm down.
"He thinks I'm killing him," she says.

> At thirteen, in the back seat of our station wagon
> outside a drugstore, watching as he leaned over
> and kissed her, I sat on my hands
> to keep from pounding his head.
> When he went in, I screamed, "You said
> you didn't love him anymore."
> You said we could move."
> She glared.
> "I said nothing of the sort."

My mother is crying. I take her hand
and press it into his, weave their fingers
together. I want to remake the past,
to close the circle smooth and bright,
but when I look again at my father
he shivers, shakes his head
and lets her hand drop.

Brother door

opens between sleep and waking, before
light suffuses sky, before I can snap shades
down, while I struggle to not remember,
not forget

memory made of lies, stories bent
to create heroes, demonize.
My eyes bear false witness.
I say I never saw

the car stop, three men in back,
one guy leering from the front seat,
patting the grey upholstery, smiling.
My friend I didn't see

hides beneath blue spruce skirt
and the man motioning from
the front of the car, her father
I never met. I ran screaming

through the back door as he hollered,
"You're not the one I want," and pulled
away. My mother held me, called the police.
Something about

not being chosen, even for what I thought
was a kidnapping rankled me, and you,
brother door, with all your hinges
oiled, ready, open

to my shape-shifting past
half remembered, half imagined,
the door I had hoped
was latched fast.

Beach Plums

After being crammed in the car for hours, we stop.
They set up the umbrella and lunch,
do what they always do. I walk
until I can't see or hear them anymore

and crouch into wild beach plums to bleed
a labyrinth of tissue down my legs—
clots and coils of unrealized body
no one sees me bend to stoop and cover.

But when my sisters come to find me
I gulp down tears and run, plunge
my grit-raw body into the ocean,
hands and lips stinging.

From the water I watch my mother
lie in the sand, oil her body to protect it.
Father threads seaworms onto hooks
and casts them out.

Water

will go where it wants
and when we try
to cut its route short, explodes
from duct-taped copper pipes
to splash the wall where the tub
used to hold it in its place.

I've seen pictures of people
huddled on rooftops, holding
each other when flood waters crest
below, bearing the swollen bodies
of dogs and children caught in debris,
floating nowhere.
It's not that water means to do it,
in fact, water wants nothing more
than to lie flat, smoothing out all
the rough edges, submerging trash,
hiding what is too well anchored
to lift and set sailing.

Water is like
your grandmother who doesn't
want to bring up the past, who
tries to keep everyone calm
when all hell breaks loose
even though, at last, she has to
pull the plug and all that water
drains away, leaves you and
your brother beached
in the center of town, drenched
to the skin and plastered

with detritus that everyone around
recognizes but won't bend down
to lift from your shoulders.

Deer Knife

When I was seventeen, a man whispered dirt
as I passed, followed me when I walked to
my job at the five and dime, sat at my booth,
took the subway I rode home sitting close,
his eyes on my breasts, his fingers shaping a
hole for his thumb to fill. I told my father.
The next night, Dad waited at the station and
when I showed up, the man circling, leering,
my father ran his deer knife across his palm,
and when I nodded, walked slow toward me,
his eyes honed on the man.

Getting to Know My Father

My father took me to a field, set cans on a stump,
fitted the 22 into my arms, told me when to pull the trigger.
I fell back with the recoil.
Dogs were for hunting or guarding the home,
not allowed upstairs
and when they disturbed by barking,
bit kids on bikes, or could not be trained
they disappeared. My father said
he put them over the fence and Rinny,
Corky, Prince and Blaze all
went that way he said, but I imagined him
pulling off the shoulder of a country road,
calling the dog to follow, positioning
the muzzle of the rifle and shooting
our failed pets dead, then burying them
so they would not be found. That was how
bad dogs went away in Missouri
when he was a boy, I figured.

Once grown, I was visiting home. My father
asked me to go with him. The police had come
about the latest dog. *You're old enough*
to see what I do. I climbed into the pick-up
gun rack mounted in the back.
The dog that bit our neighbor sat between.
We didn't talk. When we stopped,
he pulled the dog to the door of the truck.
I got out slow. The dog and Dad crossed a driveway,
stepped over a low barrier, headed
toward dark buildings, a high wall
enclosing them all. He stopped, unhooked
Franz's collar, lifted him over his shoulder,
and dropped the dog to the other side.

Lights flashed on. Countless dogs
barked, yelped, bayed. *Run!* he screamed
and we dove for the long grass,
jumped into the truck and bolted.
What was that place? I asked
when breath came back.
He lit his pipe and grinned.

Story

It could not have been true
in that faded pink room where I pasted
ballerinas on the wall above my bed.
He was headed for heaven,
the one true son, and I was just
the oldest girl who told stories,

how he stopped and never spoke
with his lips, how I hated his hands,
what his fingers said and hated
that I had to tell my mother who loved me
but didn't believe.

When my brother came home from his war,
I was fifteen and we danced
in the living room to one of my father's
old records. We danced, that is,
until my father stepped between, said,
"Son, take a shower."

So then I knew my father
was the one I should
have been telling all along.

Shadow Tag

At sleep edge, my brother,
a boy in a bird body, flees sunlight,
retreats, bolts into shadow
on the neighbor's lawn,

joins us survivors, safe
within shade's indigo,
our desert island,
where we scheme to get home

and win the game. The others,
in full sun that is sea, plot
their journey onto secure territory,
our house-shadow island

that shrinks away almost
imperceptibly as sun moves west.
Finally, we land-dwellers
find ourselves marooned

on a causeway beyond which
unforgiving light
swallows everything
and this is where I lose him.

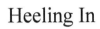

Heeling In

Cold

Just before my brother died
he invited me in—his blood
clogged with glaciers, blue wind
howling in the city of ice,
all the birds gone.

I dropped to my knees. *Is this*
what you have carried?
But he could not tell me.

Kissing Bugs

They go for the face, enthralled
by rising breath, the scent
of human exhalation during sleep:
assassin bugs, triatomines,
besucona, barbeiro, blood-suckers.

In Venezuela, Mexico, Arizona,
the light attracts, but odors hold,
entice insects close. After the kiss,
they shit parasites that seep inside
through eyes or broken skin,

ride blood rivers to the heart
and, in my brother's case, lie
undetected while he breaks
bread with other teachers
in the southwest.

Ten years later, he finds
breath short, cannot keep pace
with his new family, loses
his job, his wife, their home,
berates himself, doesn't know

what's wrong. Boston doctors
find nothing. No blame. Forty
years ago, physicians saw
symptoms: derangement,
weight loss, enlarged liver

and spleen, not Chagas disease,
but after his heart failed
and my brother died,
the diagnosis came.

Heeling In

To gain time until you had time and the season was right
you dug a slope-sided trench before freeze,
leaned raw-rooted chestnut sprigs into soil,
covered and watered.

You thought of it this way: you needed a question answered,
framed in the right words, hoped if you set
the problem in place, you'd find the best time
and way to ask.

When days warmed, before new growth showed, you spaded up
roots, set trees out, thought if I keep the silence,
separate myself from the past,
I won't have to face what could be true.

Three a.m. finds you pacing. The question lodges in your throat,
a spiked chestnut hull like those that fell throughout
your childhood, bursts from your lips:
Did my brother break me open?

Route 128

Safest car on the road, my father told my mother
as my brother and I climbed inside
the '52 milk blue station wagon.
Let's take this baby for a ride.

My brother sat behind my mother and I
behind my dad in my winter coat and
fitted hat that buttoned under my chin, the one
Mom had sewn all summer and fall

and finally removed the pins. My head sweated
within the helmet lined and lined again
until the fit met its contours.
My brother sat by the window after

drawing an invisible line dividing us.
Route 128 had just opened and
my father gunned it. Mom yelled,
Slow down, and from the back seat I watched

trees run backward, heard tires roll silent
along tar. *Doors lock from the inside,* Dad
shouted over the sound of wild air
blowing through open windows

and I looked at the silver handle, squeezed
it down. My brother smiled and waved
and when the door jerked open, I held on
with both hands, flew.

Glass

You don't want me to say
what you don't want to hear;
that at eighteen I let go my perch
on the sill and attempted to die.

A small thing, death,
when you think about it,
and common as sand, not even
remarkable anyway,

expected, prepared for or not,
but inevitable. Something
happened, though, as my rump
slid into air. I saw

the car in my trajectory, top down,
blue upholstery littered:
a stack of papers, an empty
soda bottle, newspaper

and I regretted the impact,
on this unknown car-owner

who simply chose to park
in the shade beneath a window.
But never mind. I was saved
and so was the car

but I still wonder about the soul
of things—the car's reprieve,
my skittering yank back,
and the window. Such

desperation must mark
even that liquid, the glass,
having been lifted so a body
could commence falling.

Father's Hand

His lifeline was cracked: deep crevices filled in
with black oil from the furnaces he cleaned
on his night job. The lines—streets on a map
I used to think—led nowhere and back.

Now I take the dark road to the city of his palm:
alleyways, abandoned buildings where doors bang
as wind comes up. The roads are soot-filled
and I cannot find anyone

until light, riding the air like a heron,
crosses the sky. I walk beneath a curved lintel,
stand in a room so wide I cannot see the walls.
We are many: all familiar, all staring off
in silence—we wait for dawn, I think

or for someone to tell us
why we wait. From the crowd, my brother,
straight and whole in death as he never was in life.
waves, then lifts his hooded eyes.

They are topaz beneath swamp water, flat,
and his face is scaled, reptilian.
He beckons. I step back among the others,
awake, held fast by my father's hand.

I am trying to remember

the ordering of rooms—
where my father took down walls
between stone-sinked kitchen and breakfast nook,
raised walls between self and son,

the significance of fire—
open hearths and ones bricked up
before I left worn-down shoes
in my sister's closet,

how family changed through time,
how lies and truth stood on the same
side of a cracked mirror
as each of us I am trying to remember

came to find home reshaped, remade
the first design lost—words and wood,
the ground beneath root-bound, full,
while carpenter ants tunneled through

beams, compromised the structure. I am not
trying to remember words that chafed skin,
slaps and touches, meted out
beneath cellar stairs in the dark.

Work

Father measured
cherry twice, cut, planed edges,
then planed again,
dropped skin-smooth petals
at his feet. Cautious before the final cut,
he measured once more,
taught the line between
almost and precise, fit joints tight.
He sanded last, wood dust
like pollen, sweet and strong,
then fit door to frame,
frame into space, space within
the kitchen landscape.

He expected me to follow his form:
count, weigh, reason—
but in love I forgot everything,
loved often and early, too much,
never enough, again and again
and told him, "There are no
straight lines in nature."
"But light," he smiled, "travels
straight to the mark. You can measure
time and distance as exactly as
beats of your own perfect heart
if the light's right."

Storm

Still dark—the measured tick of snow.
I rise and light the stove, blow embers red
inside the black firebox. In the night
I dreamed a white cat
thrown against banked snow on the side of the road.

My father curls between sheets, waiting,
Today the surgeon will carve his jaw away,
unroot his tongue to get the cancer.
Nurses wake him now, gently,
to put him to sleep—
                  the cat's throat
was an open gash, its mouth full of blood—

I lift the lid of the woodstove:
embers, ashes, a feeble glow
then crumple today's news and feed the flames.

Lemon Ice

He has not spoken the seven days I've been here.
Against scarred gums his tongue lies swollen and crusted.
The therapist pokes a swab into crushed lemon ice
then jabs it between his gums
like the rights he took to the jaw
fifty years before in the ring.
"He hates sweets," I tell the woman.
"It's what we use," she says. "Nobody complains."

He clamps his mouth shut and she packs up:
"When they're fed through the vein,
the tongue's the first to go. It's a muscle."
She pats him on the head. "Good boy," she says,
and pushes her cart through the door.
My father grips my hand, clenches his tongue like a fist.
I know the words.

My father

had been dying since I was born, maybe
even before, but I wasn't there to know it.
All I knew foamed in an uncapped beer bottle
in the cup holder of his van or glowed
from the pipe he held in his oil-etched hand.

He was a fighter once—welter weight
in Chicago, his shoulders and abs
all out of proportion to his narrow waist,
had to have suits made for him
for weddings and funerals, Sunday mass

where the tough guy cried at old hymns.
He said he'd never not believe; he'd seen
the marble arms of Mary move as a kid,
beckoning him, but he was oldest of 12
and it was the depression. No way

he could even begin to study God.
Besides, he'd dropped out of school
after breaking a kid's collarbone
in the only football game he ever played
and that motorcycle club

had found him and taken him on,
five guys clutching each other's hands,
a line strung across a main road on
the south side. He was a pip, my dad was,
but by the time he got to me,

he had tamed down. Just another father
doing what he had to do: two jobs,
fishing, hunting, the things he did
before Chicago. The booze was always there,
cigarettes, pipe too. He moved to Florida

and cancer, that murdering son of a bitch,
found him, grew inside lungs, jaw, tongue
and the surgeon to save him, excised
his jawbone, sent chemo into his blood
like the cavalry running down the hill

in the old westerns where all the good guys
wore white and won. I wanted him close,
to bring him home where he would not be
just one of the old dying men but have
his family to hold him.

I went down, spent a week planning
an angel flight to bring him back,
but my first night home the black phone
on my bedside table rang. The polyester
voice on the other end told me he was gone.

Dream: Edge

She drags heavy feet down the stairs
and out childhood's back hall
past the basement turn. Night crawlers lay across
the grass. At the garden she stumbles

toward the 55-gallon drum, bends
and unlaces rough brown strings, eases
veined feet out, drops each orthopedic shoe
into the drum where Father burned trash.

She slogs from the tilled garden, mud
between toes, pulls the screen door open, edges
into the back hall, turns left to go down
cellar stairs, into the windowless room below

where her brother used to sleep in his music,
the dark breathing. She opens the door.
A thin staff of light hooks into memory,
propels her backward and her feet find

cool concrete. Light haloes the workshop door.
What if her brother and her father are still there?
It has been so long since sawdust, years since
she walked barefoot, washers scattered on the floor.

What if they are boxing in the cellar, reinforce
space between supports, and have locked
all the tools away? Would they deny the foundation
that holds both their coffins and earth at bay

and how will she recognize their faces
now that decay has scrawled her name
across their lips; how remain?
How run away?

Family Noir

Shadows lunge from catalpa trunks,
slither across the lawn.

My brother, born with a caul,
falls onto a saw, jagged toothmarks
tattoo his temple.

In the breakfast room window
a bullet-size hole.

Sisters speak in tongues, tongues
and teeth and claws. Language
recoils from us.

The rectangle of missing floor
opens to the cellar.

Mother crochets storms at sea.
Cats flung to drown in burlap.
Father gulps a wee dram down.

Furnace bleeds oil into concrete—
crushed beak, stunted wings.

I leave home. Rooms shrink.
Brother, parents die. My sisters
swell—double Alices through

the looking glass—limbs
shatter windows, buckle floors.

Nantucket Sleighride

Father never said no
so they excised his lung, closed
his chest and sent him home.
For the next year his gums
oozed and each time he spoke,
his tongue found those places.
At the hospital, they said
his jaw was singing with cancer.
The doctors cut away
until the bottom of his face
was a drawstring bag
and when chemo
hurled through his veins
he squeezed my mother's hand—
held and held and held
until death took hold.
So when Mother's breath
tightened into a fist, she refused
her surgeon's pleas to slash
through tissue, burn out
tumors between, among, within
the ocean of her blood
like islands,
and she took to her bed,
narrowed to a reed,
and pumped
morphine until
she died.

Virga

an observable streak or shaft of precipitation that falls from a cloud but sublimes before reaching the ground

Rain is not falling onto branches, not reaching earth, but
evaporating, drawing heat away, leaving cold in its place,
seeding supersaturated air of impending storm.

You sat with our Mother each day until
your husband dragged you home
to care for the newborn twins, but you

would not let Mother die unfettered: *I still need her,*
you screamed, then cursed me from the outside door,
but I had turned from you

already, stepped back into her morphine drip,
her sublime stillness. You knew what I would do,
I would tell her to let go

and I did. She died that night. You locked the door
between us, washed her body down. I stood outside.
where cold air leached through the doorframe

angry that you had taken her for yourself again, angry
that even at the end of her life I allowed myself
to be silenced. I imagined

forcing the door, demanding you share your grief
and allow our tears to fall together
so they would reach into her fine strong spirit.

But each of us hoarded stones inscribed with guilt
and blame and dug them in, cold markers among
old roses and spent marigolds.

And when the undertaker came to take her,
he rolled the wheeled bed to the door
loaded the body on and eased it down the stairs.

In the dry dust driveway, you clutched the hearse
bumper, ran behind the long black car. I stayed
on the landing, unable to reach you, unwilling to try.

The rain never quenched tree roots, never came until
clouds seethed thunder, lightning flamed, and
we faced each other on the church steps.

You would not speak to me.

Divide

When Mother died, my sisters took what they decided
they were owed: proceeds from the Florida house,
furniture, the car, and finally the jewelry—
the wedding band,

two diamonds, and all those pieces I had given her:
the squash blossom necklace, silver and turquoise
bracelets, earrings. I was not there but this
is what I saw: two sisters bowed

above the habiliments of our dead mother,
choosing what to make their own, two women
broken in grief, fused in anger, resentful
that I did not give up my work, did not

take the time from my husband and children
to watch death hollow the body that had given me life.
They sent me a ring neither wanted, some wooden beads,
a hundred dollar check.

I asked them to reappraise, said I wanted only
what I had given, no cut of the real estate,
no car, no clothes, but both turned me down:
they wrote that I had given up my voice

when I couldn't get time off to sit with our mother
the long days. They said they earned
what they had claimed. I was the last to see her.
I had told her to let go.

Reflection

Where have you gone, my sisters,
after the door closed and each of us
hobbled down grand grey steps
and back into our lives?

This time of year, ice waits
in hearts of water, lies
like beads we fingered
between now and grace.

I know what's left is all I have;
don't get me wrong,
but sometimes, whys
fly against the panes—

robins flinging themselves
against kitchen windows—
and when I raise a frame

one flies inside, smashes
against the image of himself,
his beveled mirror likeness
by the door where

before her burial
just this morning
I glimpsed in my reflection
our mother's ruined face.

Finding My Mother

*Female head, Greece: Demeter or Persephone broken from
a complete figure*

Worcester Art Museum

Of course you were beautiful
but what makes you mine
is the separation, how
it leaves both of us cold.

Looking at your stone profile
I think of how the sun
leaves the world each day
and how Persephone

rests against Hades' side
below her dark winter.
My mother, your lost body
must be honored somewhere;

but I'll take this and chalk up
the loss to family, the cost
of a stopped heart, and whether
yours is the face

of Demeter or Persephone
really doesn't make a difference.
Many seasons ago your children
broke from you and each other.

I take what I can get, find
in your aquiline contours
affirmation that once
we were here together

and our bond mattered.

My fathers' jaw

was last seen two years ago in a Munich doorway.
It was nearing dark, I was on a bus tour with French tourists
I couldn't understand and in Germany, for God's sake.
It was attached, of course, to a stranger
who probably had no idea where it had come from.

I opened my journal
entered: "JAW," the date
and location under the note:
"HAIR, 2/17/02, Dublin, Ireland.

It's usually like this. I am somewhere else,
relaxed, tired from whatever brought me there
and in a crowd or passing on a bicycle is a missing piece—
the nose in Boston, his hands in a village outside Edinburgh,
his shoulders pitching hay in New Brunswick.

Yesterday I followed his bandy-legged walk
through my own home town. I'm no Isis with an agenda,
but, hey, once I get all the pieces found, I'll know where he went.
I'm closing in.

Mirror

I have outlived you, Mother, and
to be honest, can't remember your face.
I know the shape, your skin, its pores and lines,
but I was so caught inside my own body
that I saw solely through my own eyes.

Did I relinquish you
when you readied yourself for bed,
smiling at what I said happened.
Boys will be boys, you laughed. *Besides,*
you've always had quite the imagination.

How many nights did I walk railroad ties
until sun broke out, trying to find a way
you'd believe me? You couldn't know
how alone I felt and when I finally left,
I sealed the door between us.

Once we moved within a three-way mirror
as you pinned my wedding gown.
Our images repeated: daughter, mother,
down the silver passageway
and through the needle's eye
until both of us were small
and far away.

Coyote

I ease a log into the stove. It is zero outside
and the sun is not yet risen.

Yesterday, or was it the day before
I watched two coyotes eat fallen apples.

Now moonlight grazes only one set of tracks
that loops out of the forest.

So many are lost among low branches
in deep snow. Not long ago

I lost a family, one soul at a time
and the woods beyond stone walls

where in summer fox grapes climb tangles
and burrs, is grown beyond my understanding.

What lies ice-sheathed, hidden,
when we turn from each other?

If I met my sister in these woods, would I
recognize her beneath the full snow moon?

What Was Lost

A 14 karat gold rosary Mrs. Fleming found
in a restaurant bathroom and, being a
no-nonsense type, slipped into her purse
and gave to me, a neighborhood kid who
happened to be Catholic. I left it in a tree.

A silver and malachite bracelet I wore
for years that slipped from my wrist one day
when I walked the dog, drove to BJ's,
and squished across a muddy field
toward Worcester State and poetry,

the antique ebony card case I bought
between classes in Dublin but gave away
to the first man who said he loved me
and when he disappeared with it
a year later I missed it, not him;

countless articles of clothing: the other
sock, a favorite pair of brogues, jeans
holed and patched, the coat dry cleaned
away, the grey and yellow silk scarf
I wore to church the last Easter I believed,

balls dog-gone into ponds and fields,
sucked down sewers, thrown
over the fence into the grouchy neighbor's
yard, the one dug into vernal pool decay
and submerged with Jacob's sneaker,

friends of the moment, whenever
that was: childhood twins, first boyfriend,
college roommates, a couple whose hamburgers
I cooked into hockey pucks in early marriage;
family: my parents, brother, sisters,

and time, of course, the years rolled up
like logs and burned in the stove, the ones
that kept me warm and oh, the blaze
tells stories: sapphire, gold, ruby flames
indistinguishable from truth, all gone.

Questions I Never Answered

Night comes like age, invades corners of rooms
where dust links chair legs

then slides out from closet doors, down cellar steps, climbs
to attic eaves stretched beneath loose shingles.

Shutters bang. I unlock the box that holds my childhood—
grey and white photographs: Mother arm-and-arm

with some of her sisters: three girls in small hats;
my father a child in overalls sitting in long grass,

an aggie poised to knock out a round of small bright marbles;
my brother and I, his ride-on firetruck gleaming, my white cat

clutched to my chest; our small sisters in homemade dresses
standing between the sundial and fallen trees in the side yard,
the grape arbor lattice shadow darkening their faces.

Where are the words we spoke in that hurricane?
What became of marble shadows, the white cat?
How can *forever gone* ache less than presence
when we still live in the same world?

Closure

Note the rose passed hand-to-hand across
the granite stair and now that the church
stands empty, the sisters turn to stone.
Irish pennies seal the closet eyes
that used to never close.
Floodlights erase shadows between elms.
My father's ashes rest beside
my mother's crossed arms
and my brother's bones
lie alongside our grandmother.
The window glass
punctured by a hailstone
has been removed, replaced,
the lawn mowed before
grasses had a chance
to flower. Catalpa pods,
white blossoms,
trunks and branches
ground to dust.

Rue

Against the dark, words fly up—
flares on a back road
after the car smokes, shudders, stops

and stepping out,
locking doors
you wonder
why anyone would want
what is worthless—
pennies on the dash,
empty cigarette packs stuffed between seats—
the vehicle itself
out of gas, broken down,
the chassis rusted through.

Memory disables the rememberer, lifts
itself hand-over-hand, solid as shadow.

A stream pulls to tide. Water
knows its way
out of the forest.
When it widens
anything can topple in,
even you, and the current
can carry everything center.
It is easier to let yourself ride.

Let someone else decide
if you should be saved.

Invocation

I am the one who no longer
walks the path, bones browned
from the suck of earth. My
stony forefinger plucks your hair;
my lips graze gravel
between flagstones. A small
green bird displays, wings
smooth as flight. He neither
understands nor believes
in dismay, but glimmers
in the light rising
from my bones.

My eyes, my lips,
my songs I would give
if I could find my way
out of this maze
that must be death;
hedges grow thick and lush
and full on both sides of the stones.
If bones sing, hear their song,
its green trilling
between last breath
and silence.

What Can Be Saved

In the ossuary where bone sleeps on bone
a thousand songs have been forgotten.

Words have fallen away, the white jaws,
toothed or toothless, can neither open

nor close. No tongue, no voice, no breath.
A filigreed curtain of finger bones

frames the portal to the sanctuary;
death has come and gone, honed flesh

to scaffolding. We do not belong here.
Beyond these deconstructed souls,

outside these walls, water froths
over stones, sings continuously

without meaning to, without thinking.
Some rocks have washed downstream,

lie tumbled together near the bank
between saplings. Shoots of blue flag

thrust green spears up through soil
where an old wooden bridge

spans the river. When we leave here
that is where I will meet you.

Keepsake

for Pam and Bede

Let the green hills
ease the landscape of your mind,
turquoise water cleanse remorse,
round back to streams that
flow to the Tasman Sea
where you float on your back
your hair spread like sunset.

Let the song of the tui sweeten
your dreams, fill you with notes
you can hear always, secure
a place for you in the sounds
of earth shifting in her orbit.

Let the circle be of bone,
be the life you will not regret,
the curves and turnings
its rivers and back-flashing streams.

Carry with you mountains
green and slate, oceans of variegating blues,
soft grey shades and shadows of clouds,
air like breath of trees.

Where else in earth do bees reach
so deeply into gold?

About the Author

Susan Roney-O'Brien has published *Legacy of the Last World* (Word Poetry, 2016) and two chapbooks, *Earth* (Cat Rock Publications, 2011) and *Farmwife* (winner of the William and Kingman Page Poetry Book Award, Nightshade Press, 2000). Her poems have been exhibited, read and discussed as part of the Massachusetts-based 4x4 Poet and Artist Collaborative as well as published in the group's anthology, *Echo & Spark* (2017). Her work features prominently in *Scenes and Seasons of a Small New England Village* by Leonard A. Haug (2017). Susan works with international students and local writers, curates a monthly poetry venue, is a board member of the Worcester County Poetry Association, and is the summer writing series coordinator for the Stanley Kunitz Boyhood Home in Worcester, Massachusetts. Her work has been published widely and translated into Braille and Mandarin. She lives in Central Massachusetts with her husband, photographer Philip O'Brien.